7 Steps

to

Move Out

of the

U.S.

Also by Greyson Ferguson

Travel for the Soul (Even if You Don't Have One)
The Forbidden Book Club
A Photo to Die For
Humanity: Devolved

7 Steps

to

Move Out

of the

U.S.

A plan for anyone dreaming of moving away

By

Greyson Ferguson

7 Steps to Move Out of the U.S.

Cover design by Greyson Ferguson

For anyone dreaming of a better life-
It's possible.

Table of Contents

Sold a Lie

Once upon a time, there was an American Dream. If you just went to work every day, put in effort, and showed initiative, you could experience it. An affordable house, college paid for with a part-time job, have a family, all while setting a little bit aside every month. We all were given a supposed blueprint to achieve our dreams. We were told it every day in school. Our parents backed it up. As did our grandparents. Everyone told us to follow the blueprint and go to the best college we could get into. Because in the end, we would all receive back what we sowed.

We were sold a lie.

Mortgages for anything more than a glorified shack cost half a million dollars some places and well over a million in others. And the shacks? A down payment costs more than what our parents paid for their entire home. Student loan payments cost hundreds, if not thousands of dollars a month. Job salaries have long since fallen behind inflation, while entry-level positions demand years experience, all while promising fast food-level wages.

Rent for a two-bedroom apartment probably costs half of your month's take home salary, food bills are skyrocketing, and even if you can afford health insurance any sudden medical expense might completely bankrupt you. Have a pet? You better be able to afford that unexpected $6,000 surgery, otherwise they're going to put your best friend down.

If this sounds like your life, it's incredibly frustrating, but know you're not alone. I was in the exact same boat.

1

was rejected for mortgages from every major bank. I wanted to buy a fixer-upper 40K house in Detroit, but couldn't secure any form of financing. Student loans were running close to $800 a month, and rent in the middle of nowhere was adding another $1,500.

I didn't know what to do. And unless I remained permanently asleep I certainly couldn't live any kind of American Dream.

Amid COVID, with my job security flailing, I started to randomly look at any and every city in the country, trying to find affordable apartments. To discover a hidden gem where I could simply survive (because living had become out of the question).

I quickly realized that nothing inside the United States would address the issue.

And that's when it hit me. What if I moved outside of the U.S.?

Once the idea popped into my mind I dug into researching how I could move, and where I could move with my two dogs. I spent months researching, emailing, calling, and comparing. Some thought I was crazy. There were those who rolled their eyes, believing I simply wanted to go on some extended vacation from reality. I could have easily listened to them, remained at home, falling further and further under the weight of student loans and the credit cards I used to try and balance months I didn't make enough to pay all my bills. I could have listened to them and accepted the continued depression of knowing there would be no way out. Had I decided to just end it and step in front of a bus, they probably would have pretended to not know why I did what I did.

Eventually, though, we all need to do what is best for ourselves. Which is why, in the end, I made the move.

And the results? In two years, without any increase in my income, I paid off a four of my credit cards, began chipping away at my student loans, and manage to set money into a savings account to eventually buy a home back in the U.S.

That is if I ever decide to move back.

I have less stress than I can ever remember, the constant pressure of making enough money no longer weighs me down, and I don't have to deal with the bombardment of the U.S. political system and everything attached to it.

If you're reading this, then you've come to the same realization as me. That life is no longer affordable, and that you're tired of just surviving. You want to live. To experience life. Because you were not placed on this earth to be born, fall into debt and die.

You're interested in moving out of the United States. Maybe it's exclusively financial decision. Or perhaps you don't like the political climate, are afraid of surging gun deaths, or have compared medical costs to other countries and don understand why it's so much more affordable almost everywhere else in the world

Whatever has brought you here, you're in good company.

Standing there at the starting line, moving out of the United States can feel daunting. How do you even go about trying to move away from the country you've known all your life? And how can you even afford to move out if you can afford to live in it?

I am here to help you. I have lived it all, and I've done it all. And I'm here to tell you it isn't as difficult as you might think. It will take some research on your end but I'll show you the ropes and guide you along every step of the way.

ecause I want you to finally live the life you've dreamed of. It's the American Dream, just outside of the U.S.

1: Mindset

Not many people talk about this when it comes to moving out of the United States, but the reality is, having the right mindset is the foundation to a successful move.

I can't tell you how many people I've talked to who have told me they "would love" to leave the U.S., and that it was their dream to do so, but they never took single step toward making that dream a reality.

There's always an excuse, and most people use these excuses as a safety net. "It's my dream...but I can't because–" insert excuse here.

I'm going to help you address most of these excuses. First, it's not expensive. At least not comparatively speaking. If it's just you or you and your spouse leaving the U.S. you'll quickly discover it is cheaper than a month's rent. And even if you have kids it's not all that much more. This is a common excuse, but it comes from people who haven't done much (or any research) into leaving.

Basically, it costs the price of an airline ticket. And, if you sell off most of what you own, like televisions, the exercise bike you've never really used, and clothing that's been sitting in your closet for years since you last put it on, you can put pretty hefty dent into that ticket. And if you have a car? Well, that's money in the bank.

At the end of the day, 99 times out of 100, leaving the U.S. in almost every circumstance will help you save money. Unless you're moving to, say downtown Tokyo or Singapore, you're probably going to be saving some serious cash.

...e not having a remote job is another excuse.

...is is a bit more of a viable excuse, but don't let it hold you back. So okay, you ...n't have a remote job. They exist. There are lots of them. I'll talk about looking ...remote work in an upcoming section, so if you're still punching in at the office, ...rking at a restaurant, or performing another job that requires you to physically ...into the place of business, I can help point you in the direction of remote work.

...ose I've talked to who use not having a remote job as an excuse aren't actively ...king for such a job. They say it, use it as a reason to not leave, and then live ...hind its protective barrier.

...cause here's the thing. Some people are more comfortable living behind excuses. ...gives them an out. They weren't able to live out their dreams because of ...nething else.

...e reality is if you want to do something, you'll do it.

...s all a mindset. And if you're going to leave the U.S. you have to be fully ...dicated to it. It's not difficult. It's less expensive than a month's rent. Simply ...t, it takes basic preparation and planning (which I will help you with).

...s, you will leave some friends and family behind, but with social media, it's easy ...stay connected, and they can always visit you (or you can visit them with all the ...ney you'll be saving). You can video call from any corner of the world. Heck, ...u can mail postcards.

...aving family and friends is probably the most difficult mindset challenge. But ...u, and your family, ultimately want what's best for you. Some of them might ...t understand why you want to leave, even if you explain you can no longer

afford to live in the U.S., or that living in the country is causing you too mu
mental anguish.

Even if they don't understand at first, when they see how happy you are in t
end, they will come around.

So before you move forward with any kind of moving plans, you need to be in t
right mindset.

Do you really want to leave the U.S.? Do you really want to live a financially fi
life? Do you really want affordable healthcare? Do you really want to send yc
children to schools where there is no chance of them being shot (and where you
not forced to ask what active shooter protocols are in place)?

Whatever your motivating factors are for leaving the United States, you can't ha
one foot in and one foot out of the departing plane. Either mentally get in, or st
It's as simple as that.

But once you decide that yes, you are leaving, because you want a better life, th
welcome aboard!

Let me tell you, from my personal experience, this might end up being the b
decision you've ever made, and your ticket to living the life you deserve. Becau
you deserve to be happy.

2: Work

Above everything else, and one of the balls and chains that keep people in the United States, is work.

You need a way to earn a living when you move. Trying to land work in a new country is in itself a challenge. You'd need a different kind of visa, which is added paperwork (and headaches) you don't want, not to mention many companies would rather not try to hire someone that needs sponsorship to work, as this means more paperwork for them as well. Furthermore, some nations specifically require hiring from within whenever possible, which, unless you have a very specific degree or skill set, instantly puts you behind the eightball.

In short, you need to find work that will let you leave the United States.

In truth, this is going to be the most difficult task of moving. No, scratch that. "Difficult" isn't the right word. Time-consuming might be. I say this because there's no exact roadmap or schedule for landing a remote job. You could apply for and land a job tomorrow, or it might take months of searching and applying.

Thankfully, as there are other tasks you'll need to check off your list before moving you can look for work as you continue moving forward with your dream of leaving the United States. So you won't simply be sitting on your hands, waiting for someone to email you back.

Many of these other tasks will require research on your part. Some of the other tasks will require you to follow a very specific schedule (specifically if you have pets, and don't worry, we'll get to that later).

So don't fret if you don't have a remote job at the moment. More and mor companies are offering remote work, because it means they can hire someon from any pocket of the United States without paying to relocate them. It als gives the company access to a larger collection of skilled professionals.

The best way to start is to go to various job posting websites, such as Indeec Media Bistro, or LinkedIn, and begin looking for remote work. You can us "remote" as a target keyword, or you can add it to the "Location" field.

If you have a specialty that you've built your resume on it's naturally better t search for remote work in this field. Whether this means you're skilled in HR, ar a teacher, or really anything else, chances are there is a growing number of remot work positions in your field.

Your current job might allow you to go fully remote as well. Of course, it something you will want to tread lightly with. After all, some businesses might ge skittish if they discover you're looking for remote work and let you g prematurely. Basically, feel this situation out, and don't announce to the work your intentions of leaving the U.S.

You've already tackled the mindset and you know you're going to leave, but th rest of the world doesn't need to know this just yet. Don't post it on social medi either. Yes, we all love to brag about what's exciting with our lives, but sel preservation with your current job is more important at the moment.

Treat this like any other job search. The only difference is this job will open th door to a brand-new world. A world of excitement and new possibilities. It wi allow you to live out dreams you didn't think you could ever possibly experienc in this lifetime.

Don't fret if you don't land a job right away. I would highly recommend not moving out of the United States for at least six months, if not a full year after you've decided to leave. Trust me, I know you wanted to leave yesterday! But there are tasks you'll need to take care of that you won't want to rush. And I can assure you, giving yourself time to finish off all these tasks will make the move easier (and your new living experience more enjoyable).

Landing the Remote Job

Let's say you finally land a remote job. That's fantastic! One less thing to worry about. You will want to work the job for a minimum of three to six months before leaving the United States. This way you know you have a secure position and it is something you can put up with.

Depending on the country you decide to move to there will likely be several visa options for you to consider. One of the most popular visas is known as a Digital Nomad Visa. This form of visa exploded in popularity during COVID, and, year by year, more and more countries have begun to offer this visa.

Always make sure to check the specifics of the visa and what kind of paperwork the visa requires. If you are a W-2 employee, some countries do require you to have some form of written approval from your place of business that you are allowed to work internationally.

Now, chances are, if you are working remotely, your company won't care. As long as you complete your tasks and partake in any required Zoom meetings your employer most likely won't have any issue with where you are located. The company won't have to complete any additional paperwork, so it's no skin off their back.

W-2 v. 1099

We're getting into the weeds a bit here, but from my experience, it's wort
discussing. If you are a W-2 worker it means you are an employee of a company. I
you're a 1099 you are an independent contractor with specific clients. If yo
could choose between one or the other, I would suggest becoming a 109
independent contractor.

The reason I say this is because some digital nomad visas are more of a challenge t
secure if you're a W-2 worker. Specifically Spain's Digital Nomad Visa. This is
newer offering of the visa, so keep that in mind, but I don't know anyone wh
works as a W-2 employee and has been approved for the visa.

Why? Because Spain requires very specific Social Security contributions. Spain i
one of a handful of countries that do require you to pay local taxes (which yo
can deduct from your U.S. federal taxes, so don't worry, you're not being doubl
taxed). To make sure the money is going where it should, you need specifi
paperwork from the Social Security Office, and it needs your company to alte
how your SS payments are distributed. This is one of the few cases where you
employer will need to perform some different paperwork filing.

The Spain Digital Nomad Visa is unique in this case, as the nomad visa offered b
other countries isn't this particular, but it is something you absolutely need t
keep in mind (especially if you want to move to Spain). Other countries lik
Greece and Portugal aren't as specific, so you'll have an easier time as a W-
employee. I'm just here to tell you that, in general, you'll have an easier time as a
independent contractor for these kinds of visas.

3: Choosing a Destination

oosing a destination isn't as simple as twirling a globe and dropping your finger
a random country. The ol' tossing a dart at a map trick won't work either. I
n't want to bring bad news, but I also don't want to mislead you. There is a
ssibility your ultimate dream nation might be a bit out of reach. At least
tially.

ou're just looking to travel to a country, stay for 30 to 90 days, and then move
to the next destination, sure, you'll probably be able to do that, but I'm
essing that's not what you're looking for. You probably want something stable,
ere you can settle down and begin laying a foundation for your new life.

those instances, you'll need to find a way of securing long-term residency. This
ot something every country does or even makes easy. Thankfully though, there
options, and I'll help go over each to clear this process up for you and make it
clear-cut as possible. Really, it's not difficult, once you know what to look for.

terms of long-term residency, the most common options are:

- Ancestry
- Work/Digital Nomad Visa
- Retirement Visa
- Investment Visa
- Border Runs/Overstaying Visits

Ancestry

Several countries will literally give out passports if you have grandparents (or ev
great-grandparents) from the country. Italy hands out passports like Oprah givi
out swag. Other countries are similar, although the exact requirements do dif
on a country-by-country basis.

If you know you have relatives from a country you are interested in moving to
is well worth checking to see if there are ancestry opportunities. It can save y
time, and it makes finding localized work inside the given country so much easi
You won't need a work visa if you are given dual citizenship (or at least residen
thanks to a grandparent being from the given nation.

This is basically the equivalent of the amusement park Fast Pass, where you c
skip to the front of the line. Not everyone will qualify for this based on th
ancestry, but it is absolutely worth looking into.

Work/Digital Nomad Visa

I'm putting these two together although each is a bit different. A work visa me
you're able to legally obtain work from a company within the given nation. No
unless you're moving to a select handful of nations (almost all located in Weste
Europe and a few in Asia), you'll likely make more money working a remote j
located in the United States. However, a work visa is an option.

I wouldn't recommend moving to a new country with hopes of obtaining a wc
visa while you're there. This is difficult to do unless you have experience within
in-demand field (such as engineering or computer science). For this, you wou
travel to a country on a tourist visa. These can last from 30 days to 90 days, a
there likely is a chance to extend the visa once.

o, at most, you'll have six months to secure a job. And, again, unless you have a ery specific skill that is in demand, work visas can be difficult because it means dditional paperwork for the local business. Plus, many countries have equirements that state the company must hire locals first, if at all possible. Unless ou have a position secured before moving, I would not recommend relying on a ork visa out of the gate.

digital nomad visa is really where the money is. Granted, it does rely on you aving a remote position, but once you secure remote work it will be far easier to o after this digital nomad visa.

digital nomad visa allows you to stay in a foreign nation while you work a emote job from the U.S. You will need to apply for this visa. Some will want you o apply before you arrive, although, for the most part, you can almost always pply for the digital nomad visa after you have arrived and are staying on a tourist isa.

t is my experience to look up the paperwork requirements for the digital nomad isa and obtain the necessary documentation while in the States. Some common ocumentation includes an FBI background check, bank deposit information, nd possibly some official forms from the Social Security office. Once you have he necessary documentation it is almost always easier to apply for the digital omad visa once you have arrived. You would arrange an appointment with the J.S. embassy (or consulate) in the new country, and go from there (we'll dive eeper into applying for these visas in a little bit).

Vith all of this said, do note not all digital nomad visas are created equal. There re three points of interest to consider. First, how long does it last for? Some ountries allow you to stay for up to six months, others for up to a year. 'ersonally, the six-month visa doesn't do much for me. You probably can already tay there for six months on a tourist visa (after an extension).

Probably more important than the length of the digital nomad visa is whether it renewable and how many times you can renew it. Some countries won't let yo renew. I would recommend looking for a country that allows you to renew th digital nomad visa.

For example, Spain (as of 2023), offers digital nomad visas that last for a full yea You are then able to renew the visa annually for up to five years. If you stay fc five years you can then apply for residency and even receive a Spanish passpor That's a pretty sweet deal because once you have a European passport it become far easier to travel around Europe and stay longer in these given locations (tha might make up for how difficult the Spanish digital nomad visa applicatio process can be).

The last point of interest you absolutely need to consider is the applicatio requirements. Some of the requirements might on the surface look similar, bu there is a difference. Certain countries will require you to supply a letter fror your employer that states yes, that you do in fact work a remote job. If you are freelancer you naturally won't have this kind of documentation. Instead, yo typically need to have paperwork showing contacts you have with clients, that yo have worked with the clients for a set period of time (usually at least six months and that the client isn't located in the country you're moving to.

There is also often a financial threshold. You need to make a minimum amount c money or have a minimum amount of money in the bank. Basically, the countr wants to make sure you can afford to live there. Don't worry, the amount usuall isn't much. Typically it is three or four times the poverty line. If you're looking t move to a country in Europe you might need to prove you're making 2,000-3,50 euros a month. Sometimes you can have a set amount saved in a bank account an the monthly requirements are not necessary. Again, this will depend on th country, and there are a few countries that don't have financial requirements fc this visa.

Now, not every country has a digital nomad visa, although they have become more popular since COVID, so if you simply Google search your chosen country and "digital nomad visa," you'll find this out very quickly.

Retirement Visa

You don't need to always be at a retirement age to apply for a retirement visa. Some countries allow you to apply for this visa if you're 35 years of age or older. Often there is some kind of financial requirement, such as you're receiving a certain amount of money in pensions per month, or you have a set amount of money saved.

If you're like me, I assumed I'd work until I dropped dead due to all the student loans and credit card debt I'd accumulated, so a retirement visa was well out of the question (at least initially). But if you have money coming in monthly from investments, or if you have a good chunk of change saved up, it's worth checking out.

Investment Visa

Much like a retirement visa, I'm not going to go into extreme detail here. Many countries, specifically those in Southeast Asia and Eastern Europe, allow you to, more or less, buy your citizenship. It's a one-time payment and you're given a passport.

The thing is, it's not cheap. Chances are you're dropping several hundred thousand dollars, if not well into the millions. If you're like me and are looking to leave the United States because it's no longer affordable (or sustainable) this particular option isn't for you, and if you do have hundreds of thousands of

16

dollars sitting around to buy citizenship, you have money to pay an immigration attorney or an international investment banker to handle this for you.

It might be an option for the country you're looking at, but if you're reading this book it most likely isn't a financial option for you.

Border Run/Overstaying Visas

This is, by far, the easiest option, although it isn't always an available one. Basically, it allows you to stay as a "tourist" in a country for a prolonged period of time without going through all the additional paperwork.

With this option, you're not legally allowed to obtain work inside the country, but you can still work your remote gig.

So what exactly is this? All countries that either give a visa on arrival or allow you to stay for a set period without requiring a visa have a point in time when you need to leave the country. However, for some of these countries, the allotted amount of time instantly resets the moment you leave. This means you can cross the border, return the same day, and the allotted time starts over.

Once upon a time, this was how so many travelers were able to stay in foreign lands for extended periods of time. However, some of the most popular destinations have done away with the border run option. Thailand, for example, was one of the go-to countries where you could visit, cross the border over into Malaysia, maybe spend a night in Penang, and return. That is no longer the case. The same is true with other nations like Peru and Indonesia (really all of Southeast Asia has moved away from this as too many people were taking advantage of the situation).

any countries that allowed visas to reset now only allow you to visit the country
a set amount of days over the course of six months or a year.

her countries still have this option in place though. Argentina, for example,
ets your stay every time you return. But even for these countries, there's
mething you need to keep in mind. While there's no specific rule against border
as, a customs agent doesn't have to let you in. If an agent sees you're leaving the
antry every three months, only to return after a day or two, it does raise some
flags in that you are actually living in the country and not visiting. Some
ents won't care, others will.

uggest visitors to countries like Argentina leave sporadically and spend longer
an a few days in neighboring countries. It's still very affordable to visit Paraguay
Colombia for two weeks, then return to Argentina.

ow, with that said, it is worth looking into what happens if you overstay your
a. Sticking with the Argentina example, nothing happens to you. In fact, it isn't
en illegal. You just have to make sure to pay a small fine before leaving. It
esn't matter if you overstay by a few days or a few years, the fine is the same. In
t, because of this, some immigration lawyers will actually recommend this
tion because not only is it cheaper, but the fewer times you have to check in
th customs agents the better.

u will need to look this up though. A quick Google search for the country you
interested in and "overstaying visa" will give you the answer you need. Some
ve a flat fine and nothing more. Others treat overstaying visas very, very
iously (again, Southeast Asia now treats overstaying seriously).

Review

That's a large amount of information to take in, so let's summarize it quickly. T easiest way to stay long-term in another country is if some of your family is fr that country and you can apply for citizenship through them. If not, a dig nomad visa is an excellent option, and many countries don't just offer dig nomad visas, but these can lead to citizenship opportunities.

If those aren't possibilities for you or for the country you're considering, bor runs and overstaying visas are affordable alternatives if it is available for the giv country you're interested in.

Lastly, if you have money tucked away, you can buy your way into citizenship long-term stays). Some are costly. Others are affordable. The 5-year Thaila Golden Visa costs $17K, but if you sell your car and whatever else you o around your house/apartment you might be able to hit that amount (and w the cost of living being so low in Thailand it becomes a very affordable option).

My suggestion is to create a list of a few countries you want to live in. Do simply pick one and put all your eggs in that basket. Be open to three or f alternative options. Want to move to Italy? Add other locations like Portug Spain, Greece, or other similar nations to your "Plan B" list. Want Panan Consider adding Colombia, Costa Rica, or Paraguay (FYI, Paraguay is hig underrated if you want an affordable Latin American country where you'll treated like royalty because there are so few U.S. citizens moving there).

Look into long-term stay possibilities in the countries and then identify the b country for you.

4: Prepping For Your Move

So you're in the right headspace and you've picked out a new location to move to. Fantastic! Maybe you have your remote work lined up, maybe you're still working on it. Both are fine because there are still other activities you need to take care of. Some of these can be done in a few hours, others will take weeks, if not months. So break out the old Sharpie and let's start checking off tasks you need to complete before your move (turn to the end of this book for a full checklist you can cross off as you go).

Passport

This goes without saying. You need a passport. If you have one, check the expiration date. You want to have at least several years left on your passport. Maybe you don't have a passport yet, or you only have a year or two left. If you don't have one yet or it's set to expire in two years or less, apply for a new one.

Why two years? Because after living in the new country for a year you'll need to return to the U.S. and apply for a new one (many countries won't let you in if it expires in six months or less, and this might get bumped out further if you apply for some form of visa. The visa will expire when your passport does. No sense in applying for a 2-year visa with one year left before expiration). It can take a few months to receive your new passport. That's just a headache, especially after everything you had to go through to move. So take care of this now.

Banking

Don't worry, you won't need to move to your new location and open a ban account. Eventually, you might choose to, but in some instances, you won't b able to without local government identification. In reality, you likely won't nee to open a local bank account unless you decide to purchase property.

There are still some banking and financial tasks you'll want to take care of. Firs obtain a credit card that doesn't charge you an international fee for using oversea Most "travel" credit cards will not charge you this fee. It is also much safer to use credit card than a debit card.

Check your current expiration dates on your cards. If any expire shortly after yo leave you'll want to request an updated card. Receiving mail isn't always eas when you live overseas. You will be able to receive replacement cards in most Europe, but it becomes problematic in Latin America and Southeast Asia. So it best to have all of those cards taken care of before departure.

When requesting a replacement card, make sure you tell your bank/cred provider you want a new expiration date too. When I was moving I had two card expiring within six months. American Express understood the assignment an gave me a card with a new expiration date. Visa, however, did not, and just re issued the same card. Needless to say, I couldn't use the card four months into th move.

You're going to want two, if not three credit cards. Why? Because there's alway the possibility that someone steals your card information and it needs to be close out with a new replacement card issued. This happened to me. Someone starte using my backup credit card (information was obtained via a data breach) and th card was canceled. That took away one form of payment. I still had two cred cards left, but with the other credit card set to expire I was down to one for a sho period of time.

n short, have three cards if possible, just as backup payment options because you
on't know what might, or might not happen while you're living abroad.

Start Learning the Language

My language skills suck. It's one of those things I've always struggled with. My
rain just doesn't work that way. Give me six months to learn a new instrument
r to develop a new painting skill, and I'll be more than adequate in that half a
ear. But give me two years to learn a language? Better give me two lifetimes
nstead. But even so, it is critically important to learn as much of the new language
s possible. Don't rely on others to speak English to you.

ven with poor language skills, I studied and took classes. Enough so I could at
east converse with a grocery store clerk or read an entire menu with confidence.

eginning language classes as early on as possible is the way to go. I'm also going
o tell you that the free Duo-lingo isn't great beyond teaching you words.
Transitioning from the app to actual conversation is a nightmare. If you do prefer
o use software I'd recommend Rosetta Stone. However, your best course of
ction would be to try to secure a tutor from the country you're visiting.

f you're moving to a Spanish-speaking country, the Spanish they speak will likely
e significantly different from whatever Spanish you learned in high school. The
ocal tutor will help you pick up the dialect and slang better.

Now, I get it. Paying for language tutor services while in the U.S. can be pricey. If
hat is cost prohibitive then use the language apps on your phone. Try to get a
rasp of the basics. Enough to get around, ask for the bathroom, and greet people.
When you arrive in your new country you'll be able to hire a local tutor for
ignificantly less. So, if you can afford it, go for a tutoring service in the U.S., but

if you can't, don't fret. Learning the language abroad will be faster, easier (becaus it's fully immersive at that point), and affordable.

Honestly, just making yourself flashcards is a great option. That way you can pa nothing and still learn how to identify items on signs and restaurant menus.

If I could give one suggestion. When you arrive in the new country, don't alway walk around with headphones in. I tend to do that. It's a nice escape for me. Bu at the same time, I missed so much of the natural language flow I would hav heard. Picking up the cadence is extremely important in understanding th language. So, from time to time, pop out those earbuds and just listen t conversations and the world around you.

Practice Driving a Manual Transmission

If there is one skill I fully regret never mastering (or even attempting) befor moving out of the United States, it's the ability to drive a manual transmission.

In the U.S., pretty much every vehicle you buy these days is an automatic. Outsid of sports cars and a handful of no-thrills offerings, you'd be hard-pressed to find manual transmission. Now, there are good reasons for this, as modern automati transmission vehicles do receive better gas mileage. For a driving-loving natio such as the U.S., it makes sense to do whatever is necessary to boost fuel econom as much as possible.

For the rest of the world? It isn't as essential.

And the reality of it is, that just about every country you may move to relie almost exclusively on manual transmission vehicles.

ow sure, you might assume you won't be driving in your new home. That may
y well end up being the case, but there are a handful of times where driving a
icle not only is beneficial, but necessary.

ery time I've moved I've done so with dogs, and those dogs required large crates.
ally, I would have just rented a car and driven the vehicle to our eventual
tination (sometimes the city is a few hours from the airport). If I knew how to
ve a manual transmission vehicle that wouldn't be the problem. But, despite
parents telling me to learn as I grew up, I never mastered the skill.

u might be lucky and land an automatic rental. My experience though is not
ly are these rentals far more expensive, but even if you reserve the vehicle there's
guarantee it will be there for you.

you've rented a car before you know just because you reserve it doesn't mean it
ll be waiting for you. That issue is only amplified when a rental service only has
e or two automatic vehicles on the lot.

you know how to drive a stick, good for you. You're ahead of the game. If you
n't? Try to track down a friend who has one and who will teach you. It's my
perience that people with manual transmission vehicles love to be asked to help
ucate drivers on this art form.

course, if none of this is a possibility don't fret. It isn't the end of the world.
s, there have been one or two instances where knowing how to drive a manual
uld have made things easier, but it never hampered me. Only the occasional
onvenience.

ternational Driver's License/Permit

In some instances, if you do rent a car or even a scooter, you'll be able to use yo
U.S. driver's license. That, however, isn't always the case, and more and mo
countries are now requiring you to carry an international driver's license.

This is even true in moped-centric nations such as Indonesia and Thailar
Because outsiders come and assume they can handle the chaotic flow of traffic
leads to additional accidents and injuries. Simply requiring an internation
driver's license is enough of a hurdle to thin out the foreigners using vehicles.

Thankfully, this is not a difficult task to complete and it's well worth obtainin
You can even apply for it once you have left the U.S., although I'd recomme
taking care of it while you're in the United States simply because documents c
become lost in international mail services, forcing you to wait months for it
arrive (if it arrives at all).

The best way to apply for an international driver's license is to fill out
application form provided by AAA, then head to a local office with two origi
passport pictures (most AAA offices can provide these if you don't already ha
some), your driver's license, and $20.

That's all you need to do.

Phone Services, Phones, and WhatsApp

Naturally, you'll want ways to communicate not only locally but with friends a
family back in the States.

For starters, you'll want to initially have a mobile provider that allows you to
your phone internationally, but this is only temporary. It's something you can
while you set up your new mobile phone line.

would suggest going with the cheapest option that lets you keep your current phone number. I had Google Fi before heading off to South America. It actually costs me more to maintain my U.S. number for a single month than for a year's worth of mobile services in Argentina (my phone bill costs about $2 a month here).

I'll go over obtaining a new number and data services once you arrive in the new country, but before you leave, you'll want to make sure your current provider (or the cheapest provider) lets you use it internationally.

And don't just cancel your phone. You need to have an active US number for when banks and even the IRS contact you and need authentication. You can't authenticate over Skype and I've heard mixed reviews with Google Voice. So, find a mobile provider that is cheap and just maintain it. It's a little annoying you need to keep paying this monthly fee, but super cheap discount providers are often $20 or less and this will ensure you can still authenticate yourself while overseas.

As for your phone, pick up a phone that allows both physical SIM cards and eSIMs. Electronic sims are downloaded to your phone while a SIM card is the little device inserted into your phone that tells it what your phone number is. If you have a new iPhone or Samsung device chances are your phone accepts both, but you should check. Depending on what mobile operating system your device is on you can go into the System Settings, then choose the Mobile Network option. It will likely show you the option of adding an eSIM if your phone allows for this. You can also Google search your make and model phone to double-check.

If your phone doesn't allow both I would recommend picking up a new one. It's okay if you go cheap on this (Apple iPhones are more likely to be stolen, regardless of where you go and regardless of if you have an expensive Samsung. Anything Apple is usually more likely to be nabbed). If you do buy a new phone just make sure it is unlocked and not associated with a specific service provider.

The best way to get an "unlocked" phone is to buy it directly from the provider website (like Apple, Samsung, Sony, or others).

Lastly, you'll want to create a WhatsApp account if you don't have one. The rest of the world uses WhatsApp. It is a free texting and mobile service that will run off of your current phone number. If I was you I would even have your friends and family install WhatsApp for contacting you. This way you won't be charged any international long-distance fees.

Helpful Resources

U.S. Passport:
https://travel.state.gov/content/travel/en/passports.html

Credit Cards With No Foreign Transaction Fees:
https://www.nerdwallet.com/best/credit-cards/no-foreign-transaction-fee

International Driving Permit:
https://www.aaa.com/vacation/idpf.html

5: Making Connections Ahead of Time

found making real connections with locals to be one of the most challenging aspects of moving abroad. This is especially the case if you don't know anyone in the area and you don't have a concrete grasp of the language.

Learning the language will absolutely help you with this once you arrive and begin to mingle, but it's still good to know a few locals before moving. You will also want to dig up some information specific to the city, or country, you are moving to (such as locating an apartment). Try to dig into what local customs are. Do they greet with handshakes or a kiss on the cheek? Do singles live at home until they are married, or do they move out right away? Small things like this will not only help reduce culture shock but it will help you connect with locals faster. The more you know, the easier the transition will be.

For my own curiosity, I like to read through a few history books on the country, so at least I can understand certain national holidays. It's not really necessary, but it's something I enjoy doing).

If you're moving with someone the transition will likely be a bit easier. At least you'll have someone to talk to, help you out, not to mention vent to (because you will run into some frustrating circumstances along the way. Trust me). But even so, you will want to make connections ahead of time.

Facebook

First, I have a handful of easy tips and suggestions for making connections wit locals (and local expats). Head over to Facebook and search out expat groups i your chosen destination. For example, I was part of an Argentina Expat group o Facebook. This was an incredibly helpful group of people who would answe questions and provide tips. Sometimes the questions were as simple as, "How do order black drip coffee at a local coffee shop." Other times the questions wer more specific, geared towards recommended dermatologists and dentists wh speak English.

Sticking with Facebook, you should also look up apartment rental groups. Don' just stick to Facebook Marketplace. While in the U.S. this might be helpful, it isn' always as beneficial. I would suggest first looking for city-based rental groups. Yo might search "Lisbon Apartments" or "Barcelona Apartment Rentals." I'll div deeper into actually looking for, and securing, apartments in an upcoming sectio but these Facebook groups will prove helpful prior to your departure.

Dating Applications

Yes, I'm saying you need to sign up for dating apps (if you're single, of course and yes, I'm suggesting you pay for them. I know, I know, the thought of payin for Tinder in the States is kind of cringey, but trust me, setting this up befor leaving is so worth it.

When you pay for dating services like Tinder and Bumble you will be given "Travel" mode. This allows you to change where you will be matched with peopl

Before moving to Peru, I set my Bumble and Tinder profiles to Lima, Per (thankfully at the time both applications were offering this as a free service due t

)VID). While there will be some people who won't bother matching with you
:ause you're 6,000 miles away, there will be others who will absolutely want to
mect and chat.

1en I first decided to move out of the country I activated the travel feature
ybe six months out. Some of the friends I made were beyond helpful for my
ival. One even went so far as to secure a large taxi van for myself and my dogs,
well as pay the deposit to reserve it. Now, I wouldn't recommend asking
neone to pay for a service before ever meeting them, but these are some of the
st people to talk to. They can give you more of the nitty-gritty of the city you're
ing to, including what neighborhoods they would recommend and other
ider insights you wouldn't receive just by researching the town on Google.

andling Your Visa

is section is specific to anyone applying for a digital nomad visa. If you're
olying for a different visa, such as a work visa, an investment/retirement visa, or
idency through ancestry, you will want to directly contact an immigration
vyer inside the given country to help. If the country is a border-run country,
:re's no need to worry about any of this (although, depending on the digital
mad visa, an immigration lawyer might be helpful as well).

th a digital nomad visa, you will first need to determine the paperwork
]uirements. A quick Google search for "Spain Digital Nomad Visa
quirements" or "Colombia Digital Nomad Visa Requirements" will provide
1 with these basic details.

u might need to perform a follow-up search to determine if any of the
cuments need to be certified or apostled. Basically, this is a means of
:henticating the documentation to ensure you didn't just draw it up on your
nputer and print it out.

If a criminal background check is required, request an FBI background che[ck]. This can take up to a few weeks to receive. There's no way to directly expedite [a] background check, but if you are in an immediate bind, contact your congr[ess] representative and they can pull some strings. I've heard of people who ha[ve] received their background check in a few days instead of a few weeks when doi[ng] this. However, it's better to not wait until the last minute if at all possible.

In some instances, you will need documentation from the Social Security Offi[ce]. This is not common, but it can happen. As you might expect, the Social Secur[ity] Office can be...a headache to deal with, so it might take a little bit of persisten[ce]. Request the exact form the visa requirements ask for. Any kind of Social Secur[ity] requirements can get a bit odd. Now, most digital nomad visas do not request t[his] kind of information. The only visa I know of that does is the Spain digital nom[ad] visa if you are a W-2 employee. The problem with this is the document Spa[in] wants you to obtain doesn't actually exist (as of this writing, October 2023, [the] Spain visa is new, so chances are this will eventually get ironed out). Because [of] this, I have yet to see a W-2 employee obtain the Spanish visa and even [an] immigration lawyer I've talked to has said if you want to obtain this Spanish v[isa] you better be a 1099 contract worker, otherwise it's no dice.

But back to being a W-2 employee. If you are such an employee you will want [to] request a letter from your employer stating you are allowed to not only wo[rk] overseas, but specifically in the country you're moving to. If you're a 10[99] contractor, print out contract agreements you have with these businesses, wh[ich] should include dates for which you began your work relationship. Also, ha[ve] location details for these businesses. The businesses must not be located inside [the] country you're moving to. Otherwise, you need a work visa, not a digital nom[ad] visa.

You will also need financial statements proving you make at least the minimum monthly requirements. As a W-2 employee, you can provide pay slips, and as a 1099 independent contractor at least six months of bank deposits.

Some countries do require a resume, as well as a cover letter, stating why you want to live in the country. Just like writing a cover letter for a job you're applying for, the goal here is to kiss the ass of the country (without coming on too strong) while demonstrating your value. You can say things like you visited once and fell in love with the country (only say this if you have actually visited), or you've seen photographs and have always wanted to experience life in the country. Tell them about your work, how you are an outstanding citizen, and how you will positively affect the country. You know the drill.

Having copies of your degrees and other certifications can prove beneficial here as well.

If you are applying for a digital nomad visa in a country that does not speak English, you will likely need everything to be officially translated. Because the easiest way to apply is once you have already arrived in the country, the U.S. Embassy or consulate websites will provide you with translation providers they recommend. If you can't find this information scroll to the bottom of the Embassy website's main page (or select the "Contact Us" tab). Contact the listed email address and ask what translator services they would recommend for visa applications.

Now, it can sometimes be tricky to know what forms need translating, and which forms need to be certified or apostled. If you're finding conflicting information online, here's what to do. Look up immigration lawyers in the given country. Look on the website to see if they provide free consultations. If they do, schedule consultation. Tell them very frankly you are applying for the digital nomad visa, but don't know what forms need to be certified, apostled, and translated. The lawyer can assist you with this information.

If, at any time, you feel overwhelmed with this, and don't feel confident i scheduling visits to the embassy (for some visas you will need to do this, for othe: like Malta, which is performed entirely online, you don't), consider hiring a immigration attorney. These attorneys will have flat fees and will take care of a the filing, pay the filing fees, schedule your embassy visits, and walk you throug the entire process. An immigration attorney will help ensure you don't mak mistakes in your application, which saves you time, money, and frustration.

In Europe, you're looking at likely paying around 1,000 euros. The price will k less if moving to Southeast Asia or most of South America.

Helpful Resources

Visa Requirements:
https://www.globalcitizensolutions.com/digital-nomad-visa/

FBI Background Check Request: https://www.fbi.gov/how-we-can-help-you/more-fbi-services-and-information/identity-history-summary-checks

(Bonus) Moving with Your Pet

Your pet is part of your family. Where you go they go, which means where you move they will move.

That was the case with me. I had two dogs, they were my best friends, and there was no way I would ever leave them behind.

Now, if you don't have pets, you can skip this section. But if you do, this section is very, very important, because your pets may have a significant impact on where you can move. Also, when I write "you need to do this," do it. Please, for the love of all things that are good, say, "I'll keep that in mind." There have been numerous times on Facebook expat groups where someone asked how to bring their pet to a new country, and after I told them what to do, they responded with, "I'll keep that in mind," and then proceeded to not do everything I said. Months later they would then post a question and ask what to do with their pet in quarantine.

One person said they had a long layover in Peru and they were going to take their dog out for a few hours then back into the airport. I told them NO! Do not do that! Because once you're out of the airport you will need all new documentation from Peruvian authorities. But it is only for a few hours, they said in return. Doesn't matter. It could be for 10 seconds. It's all bureaucratic paperwork, but at the same time, it's designed to prevent the spread of infectious diseases in animals. So please, follow all the steps. The steps are not difficult. But skipping any one of the steps will put your pet's well-being at risk.

Do note, that this is specifically for dogs and cats. Exotic animals and birds are i their own category. You will need to check the exact requirements for the give nation based on your exotic creature. The requirements vary wildly from on country to the next, which is why it is so difficult to include generalize information about them.

High Rabies Countries

The United States puts together a list of countries it deems as a high rabies li potential. Now, this isn't to say you can't take your pet to this country. There no rule against it. The problems arise when you try to return from the country. I doesn't matter if your pet originated within the United States, it is extremel difficult to bring a pet directly back from a high rabies country.
The United States Center for Disease Control and Prevention has a list it regularl updates. Check to see if the country you're desired country is on the list (lin provided in the Helpful Resources section of this chapter).

Now, if the country you want to move to is on the list it doesn't mean movin there is out of the question. Really you have two options. The first is to move an stay until your pet passes on. Of course, there's no knowing when this migl occur, which makes it especially difficult to gauge, so I wouldn't recommen going this route.

The second option is to go to a high rabies country but plan to move to anothe country for at least six months before returning to the United States. For exampl you could move to Peru (currently considered a high rabies nation), then move t Mexico (not a high rabies nation), and remain there for at least six months. Son countries will require a rabies titer test. This means your dog has their rabi vaccine administered. Then, no sooner than a month later, a blood sample taken and tested. Such a test is usually only required when leaving a high rabi intry and traveling to certain "safe" countries. Make sure to check the quirements well in advance of leaving.

angerous Breeds

is is more specifically geared towards dogs. Certain dangerous and aggressive eds are not allowed in individual countries. It is similar to cities banning the lity to own certain breeds in the city limits.

you own a bully breed, a dangerous breed, or any other breed that often falls o this category, you'll want to search the nation you want to move to and look "dog breed restrictions" (for example, "Belize Dog Breed Restrictions").

me countries have full-out bans, other countries allow breeds with restrictions. example, your dog might need to wear a muzzle when out in public and you ght need to register the pet with the city police upon arrival. They might also uire you to take out special insurance policies for the dog.

hen moving, one of my dogs was part pit bull. This made moving challenging. at instantly took Colombia off the board for potential moves, as the breed was tricted there. Usually, if your dog is part restricted breed, or even looks like a tricted breed, they won't be allowed.

irline Requirements

is, again, is more specific to dogs considered bully breeds or "dangerous", with e exception. Does your pet have a smushed face? We're talking pugs and French lldogs (and regular bulldogs). Many airlines have specific restrictions on nsporting these kinds of dogs in luggage. This is because these kinds of dogs

already have breathing problems, and traveling at such a high altitude can ca
additional breathing issues for these kinds of pups. It's a liability issue for
airline and a safety issue for your pet.

So, if you have a smushed face pet, you need to plan on flying them in a car
within the plane. Bulldogs are where the most problems arise. While pugs a
frenchies are small enough to fly carry-on, bulldogs typically exceed wei
requirements for in-cabin transit, and they are not allowed within the cargo hol

Regardless of your dog's breed, you will want to look up airline requirements
fly with your pet. Often the airline requirements are more restrictive than
country you are flying to, so check all of this information out.

Flying In-Cabin v Luggage v Cargo

There are three general ways of flying with your pet. Inside the cabin, w
checked luggage, and via a cargo jet.

There are very specific weight and size requirements for flying in-cabin, so chan
are, unless you have a small dog, or your dog is a service animal (emotio
support animals do not count, as most airlines have cracked down on this pract
and no longer allow the dogs inside the cabin), your dog will need to fly in lugg
or cargo.

You might initially balk at the idea of putting your dog in luggage or flying th
in a cargo plane. I'm here to tell you that, as long as you follow all the very spec
kennel requirements (which your airline will strictly enforce), they will be v
comfortable. In fact, your pet might be more comfortable in their kennel th
inside the cabin. Don't worry, I'll get to kennel requirements and all of that i
bit.

The process of flying in luggage and via a cargo plane is similar for the pet, but very, very different for you.

If at all possible, you want to fly your pet luggage over cargo. In this instance, your pet will be checked in at the same time as your checked luggage. When you go to drop off your luggage, the airline staff will have you walk into the luggage area behind where you check in at the front desk. In this area, there is an X-ray machine. You will take your pet out of the kennel and the staff will X-ray the kennel. Once all is good, you will put your pup back into the kennel, and secure the door shut with the required zip-ties or locks (more on this in a bit).

With a cargo plane, your pet will use the same kennel, only the kennel will be placed on a wood pallet. The pallet is secured in the plane and the kennel is secured to the pallet. Really your pet will have more space inside the cargo plane than with anything else. But the big difference here is the cost and trying to collect your pet upon arrival.

With luggage, you will likely pay a few hundred bucks for your pet. Every airline is a bit different. When I moved from Peru to Argentina I paid about $100 total for both dogs in two full-sized kennels. But expect to pay a few hundred bucks for each pet (again, check with the specific airline for their fees).

When you arrive, you'll collect your pet right along with the rest of your luggage. From there, you will proceed to the local government inspection point within the airport. This will be the new country's version of the USDA. Inside the airport they will go over your paperwork, briefly inspect your pet, and, as long as all your paperwork is good, you'll be on your way.

Now, if you have to fly cargo because no airline will touch your dog (sometimes there just aren't any options if you have a bully breed or your dog is too big), you will have to pay a transport service provider to set up the cargo freight booking. This will probably cost you well over a grand. To fly my two dogs to Peru this ran over $3,000. I moved during COVID, so most airlines had stopped providing luggage pet transit, which is why I had to go with the cargo provider. Basically there's a good chance flying cargo will cost five or ten times the amount you would pay going the luggage route.

And that's not where the headache ends. When your pet flies cargo they won't be landing at the same airport as you. They will be flying into the cargo airport (or at least the cargo portion of the airport), and you'll need to import them like cargo. That means a ton of more paperwork, and you either need to have a very, very strong grasp of the new language (if there is one) or higher an importer.

In Peru, it took eight hours for all the paperwork to finally obtain my dogs. In Argentina, when they flew in luggage, it took about five minutes. Trust me, if you can at all fly your dogs as luggage, do it.

Alternative Transit Options

Unless you are moving to Mexico or Canada, chances are driving is not an option. This leaves you with booking a private jet to take your pet (an extremely expensive alternative method, although probably more comfortable for everyone involved), and a cruise line.

Now don't get excited about the cruise option. It's not a viable option for most people, but it's worth mentioning, because trust me, I looked into it.

Currently, the only cruise line that offers any kind of pet service is the Queen Mary's transatlantic voyage. This means you will depart likely from New York (although there are some Florida options) and head for ports in the UK. These departure and destination ports will vary somewhat, so do look up the options for the Queen Mary. If you plan on traveling to Europe and absolutely don't want to deal with flying, this might be a potential option.

our pet will need to stay in a kennel area for the duration of the trip, so don't xpect them to be allowed into your room. You'll have a small window of time to pend with them during the day, and the staff will let dogs out for small walks, ut for the most part, dogs will spend the majority of their time in large kennels. Vhich, when you consider just how long the voyage is (we're talking a week or so), 's almost better to go on a plane, if that is at all an option.

Pet Documentation

his, in reality, is the most important process if you plan on moving with a pet. ou won't have any problems, just as long as you very specifically follow the pet equirements, and scheduling, of your pet documents. The only time I have ever eard of pets being forced into quarantine is when their owners failed to follow nese exact requirements. I've advised on what to do (and what not to do), and espite this, people have "winged" it. I'm going to tell you right here and now nat you should never, ever, "wing" your pet's travel documents.

irst, your pet will need to have their rabies vaccine. Most countries have a andful of other vaccine requirements. Have these done at least several months efore departure. Many countries will not count the vaccines if they are less than a nonth old.

Vhen having the vaccines done and your vet is filling out the certifications, equest them to sign everything in BLUE ink. This is very, very important. Blue ik is required as black ink is easier to copy and forge. For some damn reason, and : makes no sense to me, many vets will sign in black ink, even when the blue ink equirement is known. So, remind them, and if you currently have the license and : is done in black, visit your vet and have them re-certify everything in blue ink. hey might question your request, but tell them you are traveling overseas and need everything in blue ink. In my experience that "jogs their memory" (ak knocks sense into them).

If I can make a suggestion, I found it beneficial to use the Banfield Vet servic found inside PetSmart stores around the country. Now, I'm not saying these ar particularly good vets (I once had a dog come back with fleas after an extended ve visit), but there are two major advantages. First, all of the Banfield locations shar information. When traveling with a pet you will likely need to book a direct fligh which means you'll be flying out of the East Coast for Europe, Miami or Housto for South America, and likely Seattle or San Francisco if heading to Asia. Ther are some very specific timing requirements that mandate you have a vet locate within the city you're departing (more on this in a second). The second benefit most of the offices will have a USDA-certified vet. Not all vets are USDA certifie (in fact few are).

By using Banfield, if there is a problem with the documents you can easily corre them because your city of departure will have a Banfield office where update information can be produced. If you only had a local vet from where you ha been living, you would need to emergency contact them, request a rush documen and pay for overnight shipping. Even then, when on a tight schedule, this migh take too long. So having a vet based out of your departure city is optimal.

But okay, let's move on. Your pet has received the necessary vaccines and you hav all the certifications signed in blue ink. You will then need to visit the USDA certified vet who will go over all the documents and perform an inspection o your pet to make sure they are free of parasites (they will also likely give your pe heartworm medication at this time). This visit must take place within 10 days o departure. It can't be further out, and it's best to do it 10 or 9 days out becaus you will need as much time as possible. I would recommend scheduling you USDA vet visit 9, or maybe 8 days out. If you schedule one 10 days out and the your departure flight is delayed by six hours, it might push your arrival time to

ys after the USDA inspection, which voids it out. So give yourself a little slack
the scheduling.

e USDA vet will then forward the information to a regional USDA office
ctronically, where this information will be certified and then delivered back to
: vet. This is not an instant process and it will take several days. I received mine
: day before departure and I had to drive 500 miles to the airport, otherwise, the
tire 10-day process would have started over had I missed our flight (which is
y I recommend having a vet inside the city you're leaving).

) note this was a unique situation as we were still in the middle of COVID, so
)cessing times were delayed. You will likely receive your paperwork back sooner.

ice the USDA vet receives the information they will both email you and
)vide you with a hard copy. Again, ask the vet to sign it in blue ink. With this
perwork in hand, you will be good to go.

o recommend making multiple photocopies of all this information. The airline
ght require some documents to keep on hand, and the inspecting agency of
ur new country might keep a copy as well. So make extras, keep hard files on
ur computer, and just do what you can to ensure you have backups (and travel
th the backups).

eparture Cities

nentioned this a bit earlier, but your departure options are a bit limited when
veling with pets. Only certain locations will fly with pets internationally out of
: United States. On top of this, there are often time restraints for how long a pet
1 be inside of the luggage hold. And, honestly, don't you want to do what you
1 to shorten your pet's time in luggage as well? So you might need to perform
ne travel with your pet to the departure city. I was in Michigan and had to

travel down to Miami to fly to South America. It involved renting a car (and a telling them that I had pets with me).

If you move with pets, your pet will be the most expensive part of the process, b if you're like me, you would spend the extra bit of money to accommodate them

Kennel

Once you hone in on an airline you will want to check their pet ken requirements. These are generally universal, but some have some sub differences. However, I can give you the basics so you have a gene understanding of what to look for if you're just shopping around.

First, your dog needs to be able to stand without its head hitting the top. It a needs to be able to freely turn around in the crate. The airline will give you ex measurements for this. Never once did I have anyone come out with a measuri tape, but they will just check to see if your pet is comfortable (as comfortable a pet can be in a kennel).

Your kennel will be two large pieces of thick plastic held together in the middle a series of screws. The screws that come with the kennel, even the high-end on will almost always be plastic. These are no good. You need metal screws. You c order dog kennel screws from Amazon for only a few bucks.

While you're ordering the metal screws, purchase four luggage locks (the kind t has the metal wire that comes out the top and then snaps back). Some airlines w require you to secure each corner of the kennel door with one of these loc Other airlines will require a zip tie. Best to have both on hand when you head to the airport.

peaking of zip ties, the corners of the kennel will need to be secured with an individual zip tie. There is a hole punched into every corner where the top and bottom halves connect, so securing a zip tie around each is easy. You will want to purchase a plastic food and water dish that clips onto the kennel's metal door. Any free-standing dish will not be allowed.

Inside the kennel, you will want a thin cushion. I picked up one that was about an inch thick and was made with orthopedic padding. On top of this, you will then need to place a dog potty training pad, in case your pet has an accident during the trip.

You should also pick up the "Live Animal" stickers with upward arrows off of Amazon. There are sets you can purchase that not only come with these stickers but with name tags where you can write in contact information. If you decide to book a pet shipping service they will have these for you, but if not, you will want to have them. The airline website will have instructions on where to place the stickers. You should then use packing tape to secure the stickers further. Some of the glue on those stickers isn't all that great, so extra tape is helpful.

Lastly, when you take your pet to the airport, bring a ziplock bag of their food, a water bottle, and some extra zip ties. The airline should let you secure the water bottle and bag of food right on top of the kennel. This is so that, in the off chance there is a delay, the airline staff can pour food or water into the food/water dish attached to the kennel door.

Your pet will not be allowed to wear their collar inside the kennel, so roll this up and either carry it with you or secure it to the side of the kennel with a zip tie (that's what I did). Additionally, pets must travel separately (as in not two pets in the same kennel). Air travel can make pets anxious and there's no telling what it might cause a pet to do, so in almost all circumstances, pets will need to have their own individual kennels.

A Few Last Tips

First, have your pet microchipped. Some countries require this, others don'
Regardless, do it, and make sure the address is registered inside the United State
This will help when you return to the U.S.

Second, have your pet's nails trimmed before you go. The one issue I had (outsid
of long paperwork) was, apparently, at some point in time, one of my dogs had
nail caught in one of the metal grate windows and ended up ripping the entire na
off. I'll never know exactly what happened, but you better believe all my dog
receive proper mani/pedis before any travel now.
Lastly, relax. Your pet is in good hands. The luggage compartment receives th
same temperature control as the main cabin, so it will be comfortable for them (
still like to tell the staff I have a pet in the luggage compartment when boarding
just to make sure the captain turns temperature control on before takeoff). An
with all the new kennel requirements for international flights, there's no chance c
them getting out.

If you're worried about your pet's anxiety, talk to your vet about anti-anxiet
medication. You don't want to knock them out, as this can cause problems wit
their breathing, but anti-anxiety medication is great in that it chills them ou
(basically they're having the best high of their life).
And, you can have a small toy inside the kennel for your pet. Don't put any har
plastics or toys with squeakers that could become lodged in their throats. I als
tossed in a worn t-shirt into the crates, just so the dogs would have my scent wit
them when they traveled. If you have an underwear-loving dog, toss in som
tighty whities. It's all about helping your pet feel comfortable and reduce the
anxiety when traveling.

Also, not all dogs like kennels (or at least aren't used to them). It's best for you t
purchase the kennel early on, then leave it open and on the floor so they can acce:
it. Place bedding in there so it is comfortable. They might begin using it on the

wn. If not, I personally began placing my dog's food dishes in the kennel, so
hen it came time to eat they had to go in. This helps acclimate them, so when it
time to fly it is less stressful (and even comforting).

Helpful Resources

CDC High Rabies Countries: https://www.cdc.gov/importation/bringing-an-
nimal-into-the-united-states/high-risk.html

Banfield Pet Hospital:
https://www.banfield.com

Find a USDA Certified Vet:
https://www.aphis.usda.gov/aphis/ourfocus/animalhealth/nvap/ct_locate_av

6: Finding An Apartment

You have your one-way plane ticket all booked. Just saying that is pretty exciting isn't it? It makes it so much more real. You have a ticket with no plans on when you'll return.

Now, chances are you have at least a few months to figure out your next move which is finding a place to stay.

This should be done in a few steps. And, of course, I'm here to help you with it.

Extended Airbnb

Normally I don't recommend Airbnb. The platform has, simply put, caused too many housing issues, not only in the United States but often even more so in other nations. However, for month-long stays in other countries, this will be the best starting point. Call it a necessary evil if you will.

There's one thing to keep in mind. Airbnb's around the globe are gobbling up apartment space from locals, which is causing many to move out of neighborhoods they have called home for decades (or generations), which pushes them further away from their work and schools.

This is a major reason why I try not to stay in Airbnbs whenever possible. However, In your situation, it really is your only option (that or staying in a costly hotel for weeks, if not a month), but you need to do your part to protect the local nomy, not alienate its residents. Them being forced out due to overpriced rtments is no different from you leaving the U.S. because it is overpriced.

what can you do? Look up the host of an Airbnb you are interested in. See if y own or manage others. If you find someone is managing several, if not zens, of apartments, don't book with them. They are a big part of the problem. tead, book with someone who has just one spot.

ren booking the Airbnb, you'll want to give yourself time to find an apartment. is can take a while. Trust me. When I first arrived in Argentina I reserved an bnb for six weeks. I had to extend my booking an additional five days to secure apartment. Now, it did take longer because I had pets, but be aware this cess is often far more complicated (and more of a headache) in other countries n it is in the U.S.

ry? I'll get into that in a bit.

art Looking For Apartments

u can start looking for longer-term apartments while in the States before your parture, but you shouldn't secure one until after you've arrived.

re reality is, that it is difficult to impossible to know what actual state the rtment will be in, and you don't want to wire any money. Pictures can be ctored, or, if the camera was to just pan to the right a smidge, it would show a ssive hole in the ceiling. Never fully trust photographs or the agents trying to nt you the space. Plus, I've heard enough stories of people sending money fore traveling and signing a contract only to arrive and discover the landlord iped their money, rented the apartment to someone else, and won't return any ls or messages. Other times I've heard of people arriving to missing appliances,

AC units that don't work, and so on. You're just better off spending a little m⟨⟩ on an extended Airbnb stay while you look for a new apartment.

That doesn't mean you shouldn't search around and get a feel for w⟨⟩ apartments are renting for in the area. There are a few options for those. ⟨⟩ starters, search Facebook for apartment rental groups. Now, I don't m⟨⟩ searching Facebook Marketplace. You can if you like, but I've had much m⟨⟩ success with joining Facebook groups populated by local leasing agents (look ⟨⟩ "Paris Rentals" or "Apartment Rentals in Lima" within Facebook and search ⟨⟩ available groups).

You can try Google searching "Apartment Rentals in Lisbon," but this is going ⟨⟩ be a bit hit and miss. Sometimes you will find websites that are similar ⟨⟩ Apartments.com. I say hit and miss because often these websites are not upda⟨⟩ regularly. Agencies must pay a per-listing fee, and many won't want to pay this.

When I first arrived in Argentina I used such a website. I found a dozen or ⟨⟩ apartments I liked, walked around the city looking at the locations, and t⟨⟩ began to reach out to the listing agents. I discovered not a single one was an act⟨⟩ listing, and many had been off the market for over six months. Talk ab⟨⟩ wasting time. Between looking at apartments, contacting agents, and waiting ⟨⟩ them to reply, this was two to three weeks down the drain. Not great when ⟨⟩ Airbnb rental days are ticking off.

This is something you can try though. If you find an Apartments.com-⟨⟩ website for the city you're moving to, select a few apartments you like (while s⟨⟩ in the U.S.), then message the listing agent. Find out if they are still available ⟨⟩ they are, great, the listings are updated. But if they aren't, I would suggest look⟨⟩ at the listing agent's profile. It will show what real estate company they work f⟨⟩ You can then go directly to that agency's website for updated listings.

And yes, most rental properties are managed by real estate agents. This means, unfortunately, you're likely going to pay a "listing fee." More on that next.

One last thing on this. When messaging an agent, you will almost always have better luck if you text via WhatsApp. Email is...not always the best contact point. Do you know how many emails I had responded to while living in South America? A grand total of zero. You can try email while in the States if you'd like, but more often than not, WhatsApp is the way to connect.

The Cost of Entry

Every location is a bit different. However, if you are dealing with a city where most apartments are handled by listing agents, you will likely need to pay a listing fee, a security deposit, and a month's rent. The security deposit is worth a month's rent, as is the listing fee.

Yes, this is a pretty steep price, especially when the real estate agent doesn't do much (thankfully, in many locations, rent is a third, if not a quarter of what you pay now, so even when you lump those three fees together it might only cost what you'd pay for a single month's rent back home). For me, the real estate agent is the worst part of the entire ordeal. My experience has been that it's almost like herding goldfish. Trying to keep their attention and checking in (finding an apartment might be the most annoying part of moving) is a job in itself. So basically that month of rent is paying them to show up with a paper contract.

If you don't have a firm grasp of the language, make sure you have Google Translate on your phone. The app has a camera feature that allows you to snap a photo of a document and it will translate it for you. The translation can be a little rough, but you'll at least know what each section is about. Focus on who is in charge of repairs. You or the owner. You'd be surprised how often the owner takes on this and pushes responsibility to you. Always point this problem out and request them to change it in the contract. If they don't, I'd consider walkin away. Appliance repairs, unless it's your fault, are not something you should b forced to deal with.

Of course, that's just me. If you really love the location, appliance repair b damned, go for it. Just know if something goes wrong, you'll likely be responsib for ponying up the cash for a repair.

Features

Be very specific when it comes to the features you're looking for in an apartmen If you have a pet, be upfront with this. I know in the States you might want t hide the fact that you have a cat because you don't want to pay that pet deposit pet fee, and monthly pet rent (even though the kid next door causes way mo damage than your cat). But this is a different situation. Tell them you have a p so then the leasing agent can provide you with apartments that are pet-friendly.

Also, be specific about what appliances or features you want. When I moved in wanted it to be furnished with all utilities included. Signing up for utilities an Internet can be a bit tricky as a newcomer, so it's just easier for the landlord to pa for these and then you pay a bit extra if you go over the allotted energy levels. A of this makes life so much easier, and you might be surprised how affordab energy can be in some locations (in many countries energy is subsidized by th government, so you're paying a fraction of what you would in the U.S. Again, th is location specific, but you'll likely save a pretty penny).

I personally think finding a furnished apartment to start is the way to go. Th allows you to get the feel of everything, and it makes it easier to move if yo decide you want to try out a different area of the city/country/world.

Do note, however, that not all appliances you find in the U.S. are going to be available in other parts of the world. If you're going to Europe, not everywhere has AC, although I'd still try to find it, because some of those European summers can be brutal. However, finding an apartment with a dryer is almost impossible. Most countries hang their clothes up. So that's something you might need to get used to.

Whatever you're looking for though, just make sure you are upfront about it.

Be Prepared to Walk

While you should absolutely love the apartment you choose, don't fall in love with it until you have the keys in hand. Weird things can happen.

One time, I found an absolutely perfect apartment. I signed a lease and paid a reserve fee to secure the apartment. I would pay the rest of the money on move-in day. About five days before the move-in, the real estate agent contacted me, saying the apartment owner had changed his mind, and now wanted to charge me three times the security deposit.

Excuse me?

I asked why, and he said because I had dogs. Me having dogs was already known, I responded. This wasn't new information and, in fact, I had text messages confirming the real estate agent had discussed it with the property owner. The agent told me it didn't matter, the owner wanted to charge me three times the security deposit. I could take it or leave it.

So I left it.

This was an obvious ploy to ring me out for extra cash. Many locals told me wha[t] they had done was illegal, and that as I had already signed the lease they could n[o] do that. But the reality was, what could I do? Try to take them to court? We a[ll] knew that wasn't going to happen. They just thought I would pony up the cas[h] and continue the move-in.

I didn't. I passed, started a frantic apartment do-over search, and ended u[p] somewhere else. Unfortunate, but I wasn't going to let them take advantage of m[e].

Because here's the thing. If they know they can take advantage of you right out [of] the gate, there is no stopping them from doing it again. And again. And again.

Maybe you're not someone who regularly stands up for yourself in the States. Yo[u] default to others. You don't mind being taken advantage of a little bit if it mean[s] an awkward situation will end sooner rather than later. I'm here to tell yo[u] moving out of the States and being on your own (or mostly on your own) i[n] another country will strengthen your spine. Because, oftentimes, you will hav[e] nobody else but yourself to depend on.

This isn't meant to frighten you, it's meant to invigorate you. You will learn ne[w] things about yourself. That you can depend on yourself and that you can get b[y] without needing anyone else. Sure, help and having someone else around is alway[s] great, but you will be so much better for this experience, whether it is short-ter[m] or permanent.

But back to the apartment. I just want you to know that it is okay to walk away [if] they start pulling outlandish moves or going against what you've signed up for (o[r] what you're comfortable with). It might put you in a temporarily tight spot, bu[t] you will move on and find something else.

yeah, I just mentioned being taken advantage of in the last section. Those are
: major situations. Chances are though, you will be somewhat taken advantage
regardless.

st, you're an outsider, with perceived money (because you're an outsider), so
:n the nicest seeming people will probably try to take advantage.

u need to educate yourself on what apartments are generally going for, and
1at the standard practice is for agent fees and security deposits. Every place is a
different. Thankfully, you should figure this out along the way as you look
:r apartments and contact agents. You'll become accustomed to what most of
: apartments are charging and what kind of fees are attached.

ou have made some friends on the dating apps or through the expat Facebook
)ups you can ask what sort of fees are likely. This is an instance where the expat
)up will be a bit more helpful. Locals will rarely pay as much as you. It's just
w it is. They also will likely rent out unfurnished apartments. You can work up
that eventually, but just starting out, as you get your feet wet, the furnished
artment is the way to go.

is means the issues you're facing your local friends might not know anything
out, but your Facebook expat groups will.

)w, with that said, if you managed to make some local friends before arriving, it
1 be very beneficial to bring one of them with you when looking for apartments
d talking with agents.

7: Settling In

You have your apartment!

You signed all the paperwork, received your keys, and now you have your feet ᵘ toasting yourself to moving into a new apartment in a new city in a new countr

How do you feel?

I bet you feel pretty good. It's a pretty big step! You have your job, you've flo across the globe, and now you have your apartment. That's all of the big stᵘ Congrats!

Sure, you'll have some other odds and ends to take care of, but don't woɾ That's all small potatoes compared to what you just accomplished.

Give yourself a day to pat yourself on the back, because you deserve it, aᵘ tomorrow, we'll set out on handling all the other tasks you need to polish off complete your move. Getting your apartment was a big one. One of the biggest

There might still be one last big thing to tackle (specifically visa-related), anᵈ bunch of minor stuff.

Some of these minor activities you can take care of before moving into yᵒ apartment because there will be some downtime. But just to make things easⁱ I'll group them all here and you can cross them off as you go along.

You might have the desire to try and use the SIM card and mobile service from the United States. Maybe your mobile provider promised you some kind of international plan or that you can use your device at no extra charge anywhere in the world.

That will only work for so long, and you're probably going to be overpaying.

I signed up for Google Fi specifically because it advertised itself as an affordable international service option. For a while, it worked. But, after a few months, I received a message saying basically it was obvious I was no longer in the U.S. and that my data access would be shut off entirely. I could still make phone calls and send texts, but I couldn't use data. Kind of important.

Regardless of your provider, you'll want to pick up a local SIM. I almost always use a pay-as-you-go local SIM. This way, I just reload the plan every month. It is affordable, and it doesn't lock me into anything long-term. Maybe if you decide to pursue residency in the new country you can go for something a bit more concrete, but when settling, a local SIM with pay-as-you-go service is perfectly fine.

How do you get a local SIM? It will depend slightly on where you are. However, your best option is to just go to a local wireless service provider and ask for one. They might give you one for free, or they might charge you a buck or so for it. The SIM will come with instructions on how to set it up. You can also ask them to set it up for you. I'd recommend going when it's not busy (usually earlier in the day and an hour or two after lunch). If it's not busy the staff will be more likely to help you out.

If you use a physical SIM in your phone make sure to keep the one you have, so whenever you visit the United States you can pop it back in.

It is a good idea to maintain your US phone number. I would suggest switching to a discount mobile provider. As I mentioned earlier in the book, this is because with some mobile banking services you perform, you will still need a US phone number.

What I do is I have a phone that accepts both SIMs and eSIMs. I have my U.S. number on eSIM and my local number on the physical SIM. This way I can still receive texts and calls from people back in the States while being able to access local data.

If you find yourself in a bind, your US number isn't working, and you haven't had a chance to pick up a local SIM card, don't fret. Find a spot with Wi-Fi (McDonald's almost always has this. No matter what you think of the franchise, McDonald's really is a lifesaver at times). Download Airalo. Once you create an account you can purchase an eSIM for the country you're in. Most of the eSIMs are temporary and will last from a few days to a month. This isn't a long-term solution but it does work fine in a pinch.

Visa Requirements

Depending on the kind of visa you are or aren't going after this is something you will want to put in motion sooner rather than later. Some digital nomad visas you can apply for before arriving in the country, although it often is easier to complete all the necessary paperwork while in the country.

Just make sure you know what the requirements are prior to flying out. Some visas do require you to have a background check performed in the U.S. An FBI background check isn't difficult to obtain, and it isn't all that expensive either (under $20). Now, you might need to have that background check translated into the new language. The translation can be done in your new country, so you don't

eed to worry about that prior to leaving. Just look up the visa requirements
head of time (this also helps ensure you know you can apply for the given visa).

This is another time where posting a question on the expat Facebook groups can
elp. You can feel out what others would do or have done in the past. As I said, it
ften is easier to apply for the visa in person as long as you have all the paperwork
1 hand.

The paperwork is typically pretty boilerplate. Such as proof of income (such as
nancial documents, bank documents showing deposits, and anything else that
emonstrates you make enough money), signed contracts with your employers, or
 you are a freelancer proof that you have worked as a freelancer for an extended
eriod of time. Having copies of any degrees can be helpful (especially elevated
egrees) as well (we went over most of this in the previous sections).

With all your paperwork you can then fill out any digital forms online, or go to
he U.S. embassy in your given country. For example, if you wanted to obtain a
igital nomad visa in Spain you would need to make an appointment with the
J.S. embassy in Madrid. There is a consulate office in Barcelona, but this location
oesn't handle visa applications, so you would need to travel to Madrid. It is
ifferent in each country, so check to see where you need to go for this application.

The application is pretty straightforward, they might ask a few questions, and
ou'll provide all the documentation. Make sure to fill out all forms correctly,
therwise, you will be rejected and you'll need to correct these errors and re-apply
and pay another application fee).

This kind of filing generally doesn't take terribly long. Maybe two weeks. It can
ake less time or more, it is hard to tell, but that's a good ballpark. I would
ecommend doing this early so you don't have to fret over it while you're in the
ountry for the allowed amount of time on a tourist visa (typically 60-90 days).

The embassy will take your passport while everything is being processed, so don worry when you are requested to hand it over. It just means you won't be leavin that country until the application has been approved or denied.

Signing Up For A Gym

Not a gym goer? Feel free to sprint on by this little section. But if you're intereste in signing up for a gym membership at your new location, do note there is a goo chance you will actually be required to have a doctor's note.

Yes, an actual doctor's note saying you're healthy enough to workout. Or, mor specifically, that your heart won't explode while on the elliptical. I've run into thi in Europe as well as Argentina. Peru nobody ever asked me, so it just depends.

When you arrive to sign up the gym will inform you of whether this is necessar or not. If it is, ask the gym for a suggested doctor. Typically you don't need a fu physical. You will go to a cardiologist and they will perform some basic tests o you. The times I had to go, the tests took about five minutes. I couldn't spea medical Spanish and she couldn't speak English, but it wasn't a problem.

After you pass you'll receive a health certificate, which you will then take to th gym. It's an added step, but it isn't a difficult one. And it's always a good idea t make sure your heart is pumping adequately.

Just know you'll probably need to repeat this process every year when it come time to renew your gym membership.

Helpful Resources

Airalo International eSIM: https://www.airalo.com

Give It Time

an ideal world, everything will work out perfectly. You move, you fall in love
th your new location, and that is that.

lly, as you already know, life isn't perfect. It also isn't always greener on the
ner side either.

e been to places, many places really, that I thought I'd love and, in the end, just
ln't connect with.

s impossible to forecast. I will very openly admit that, despite spending more
ne in Argentina than any other country in Latin America, I found it easier to
nnect and make friends with people in all the other countries I visited and
yed throughout the region.

nade friends in Paraguay after visiting for six days. I connected with another
rson in Chile after being there for 10. I made friends with Brazilians before ever
iving in Brazil. But Argentina? I lived there for three years and, well, the next
ne I return I don't have anyone specific I need to connect with during that
urn.

course, other people have completely different experiences. And that, right
ere, is the reality of life. We all have different experiences, and what works for
e person might not work out for you.

t that doesn't mean you should bail right away.

It is going to take some time to acclimate to not just a new location, but a n[ew] way of life. People will act differently. Sometimes it can be charming, and ot[her] times downright frustrating. It's like a dog walking through a new neighborho[od]. They will want to stop and smell everything because everything is so new! It w[ill] take two and three times as long to complete that same walk, but they need[to] absorb all the new smells.

You need time as well.

So, after a few months, if things aren't working don't pull the plug. You n[eed] some time to meet people and connect.

Maybe you didn't have luck meeting people via dating apps before arrivi[ng]. That's okay. Check out that Facebook expat group I told you to join and [ask] about local events. Wine tasting or dancing classes. Maybe movie nights or und[er]-the-radar restaurants. These are little things that will help connect you with [the] culture while also opening you up to other people.

You should try and take part in some of those expat meetups. There is als[o a] service called Mundo Lingo, which is held in major cities around the world, wh[ere] you show up, slap on a sticker that says what languages you speak, and min[gle] with others in a similar situation (this is generally a younger crowd, but it's sti[ll a] nice way to meet people).

You've already pushed yourself out of your comfort zone. So why should y[ou] stop now?

But Don't Force It

There is a time to know when to move on though. I would say give yourself a year. This lets you go through all the seasons while giving you time to try and make friends and connect. But, perhaps it just doesn't work out.

This can be difficult on its own, especially if you don't make many friends. I'll admit it. While living in Buenos Aires I became very, very depressed. I didn't have any friends other than the dogs. For whatever reason, I did not connect with the locals (and the locals didn't connect with me). Walking around a city for a year without friends is difficult.

Had I been able to, I would have left. But I was in the middle of a Master's Degree college program (the program was based in the U.S., figured I should improve my job credentials while saving money living abroad), plus moving the dogs would take additional work. So, I stayed until I completed my college classes.

Don't be afraid to, after enough time passes, go to another location. Now, this doesn't mean you need to go back to the U.S. I bet you have other locations you might be interested in. Maybe Spain didn't work for you, but what about Portugal? Greece? Malta? You could try a different continent altogether.

Don't force yourself to stay longer if you're not happy. Because, chances are, you moved out of the U.S. because you weren't happy, didn't have the money, perhaps didn't feel safe, or just wanted a new experience.

I'm here to tell you that sure, the grass isn't always greener on the other side, and there's probably no perfect city, but there is a place out there that is a beautiful fit for you, your personality, and your needs. It might just take a try or two to find it.

Helpful Resources

Mundo Lingo: https://www.instagram.com/mundolingo/

You Did It!

That's right. You did it! At the beginning of the journey, you were someone with a dream. Someone who wanted to better themselves and find a way to finally live life the way it's meant to be lived.

If you want financial freedom from massive debt, rent, student loans, and credit cards, don't worry, that will come. With the money you'll be saving, you'll finally have the opportunity to pay off some of that debt and stretch your financial wings.

If you wanted an escape from American politics, or from wondering when the next shooting might take place, you're already experiencing the benefits in your new country.

Or maybe you just wanted to experience life with reduced stress and a new way of living.

Whatever your motivations were, whatever your reasonings, whatever pushed you to this point, you've done it!

At the beginning of this journey, it felt like a long road. You might have felt overwhelmed. Moving out of the United States can be stressful, and time consuming, and there might be some hoops to jump through (depending on your desired destination), but it doesn't need to be difficult.

hope, at the very least, this book has helped you along the way. I've put in everything I could think of that would help alleviate some of that stress and give pointers to help avoid some of the pitfalls I experienced.

Now, this doesn't mean there won't be some bumps along the way. After all, we all must take a unique path, and your road will undoubtedly be different from mine. But now, finally, after months of planning, researching, taking pets to vets, checking plane flights, practicing new languages, and connecting with locals in the new destination, you have done it.

Congratulations! You should be proud of yourself.

Not everyone is willing to do what you just did. For one reason or another, they will remain back home. But not you. You took a leap of faith and will be better off because of it.

So enjoy yourself, and live life to the fullest.

Because after all, there's only one life to live.

FAQs

Q: Can't I Just Teach English?

Can you? Sure. Should you? Eh, probably not. Here's the thing about teaching English in another country. First, there are already a ton of people doing this. Second, and the bigger issue, is you will be paid in the local currency at the local rate. In other words, you're going to receive very little for your work. You might have housing covered (which is normally in a shared space), which is alright, but the amount of money you receive makes it difficult to do much of anything. And if you have debt to pay off? It'll never work.

So, yes, you could teach English, but unless you already have savings and next to no debt, it isn't a viable option.

Q: Do You Need A Return Ticket?

So remember how you bought that one-way ticket? Okay, so there's a sligh chance you might need some kind of ticket showing you're "leaving." If you pla on applying for a digital nomad visa while you're in the country, will perforr border runs, or you're in a country that has a flat fee for overstaying, som locations do want to see a departing ticket.

This happened to me all the time when flying back to Argentina. However, it wa never Immigration that asked. Instead, it was always the airline I was flying witl And I couldn't just tell them I had a departing ticket. I needed documented proc (such as a screenshot or an email confirmation)

what are you supposed to do? Just buy a random ticket and swallow the
ꜱenses? Not necessarily. First, if you're traveling to Europe you won't really find
s to be an issue. If they do ask, just say you're going to depart via train.

t there are some options to consider. First, you can purchase a refundable ticket
the cheapest international destination the day before you depart, then request a
 und once you arrive. Yes, that means some credit card money will be held for
ꜱybe a week or so, but hopefully, that's not an issue. You can also purchase a
s ticket to a neighboring country. That probably won't be refundable, but it
ely will cost a fraction of the upfront price of an airline ticket, so if you don't
ꜱe the available credit card balance space, this might be a viable option.

ꜱw do you know what will happen for the country you're traveling to? I suggest
pping this question in the Facebook expat group you're in. Just enquire if you
ed to show a departing ticket when visiting. If, on the off chance you're stopped
the airport and they won't let you continue until you have some proof of a
ꜱparting ticket, you can hop on your phone and purchase a bus ticket, then
urn to the check-in line and show the agent the receipt.

ꜱ Do I Need To Renounce My Citizenship?

ꜱ, not at all. This is not something you ever need to consider. At least not for a
ꜱile. The reality is you only should consider renouncing your citizenship once
ꜱu have established citizenship in another country, you have no plans on ever
urning to the U.S., you have a foreign job, and you're so disgruntled with both
ꜱ United States and paying taxes that you want to completely sever ties. Because
ce you do, there's no turning back.

t to leave you don't need to renounce anything. It is very possible to live in
ꜱother country while maintaining your U.S. citizenship. The U.S. passport is

very powerful, and chances are, if you decide to live in another country long te
you will be able to obtain a second passport (this isn't a hard and fast rule, l
you can often carry both a U.S. and European passport).

So there's no need to renounce anything, and that is a very serious considerat
far down the line.

Q: Do I Need To Pay Taxes?

Yes. Sadly, this is one thing you'll never get out of (unless you do renounce yo
citizenship). Now, you won't have to pay state or local taxes, which is nice, l
you will always need to pay federal taxes. This is something to look into. Ma
nations (specifically European) have agreements with the United States, so if y
are required to pay European taxes all of that is taken out of what you would
back to the U.S. This, thankfully, prevents you from being double-taxed.

The tax agreement, however, isn't the case for every country. Some countries v
tax you even if you are working a digital nomad job that's based in the Uni
States, and if the country doesn't have an agreement with the U.S., you will
the full tax rate to your new country IN ADDITION to the full federal rate to
U.S.

This is absolutely something to look into. It's an easy Google search, so look
"Does 'insert desired country here' have a tax agreement with the U.S." I
example, if you were to go after the digital nomad visa in Spain you would have
register as a freelancer, and then pay a Spanish income tax. However, when y
then go to pay your U.S. taxes, you can deduct this (just make sure to file yo
Spanish tax return first). It does mean some extra tax paperwork, but at le
you're not being double-taxed.

Q: How Can I Watch All My Favorite Sports and TV Shows?

This was one of my big concerns too. I don't know if I would have moved if I couldn't watch all my favorite sporting events (just kidding. I still would have, but listening to a radio stream wouldn't have been the same). While, no, chances are you're not going to find some bar that carries everything (although some spots will have NFL and NBA packages), you can still watch them in the comfort of our own home.

How? Subscribe to a VPN. This VPN will hide your current location and make it look like you're anywhere else in the world. I use NordVPN, but there are other options out there. If you look around there's almost always a nice subscription discount, and if you order through an online shopping portal like Rakuten you can usually receive a large percentage of that purchase back in your pocket. I do a lot of my online shopping through Rakuten. There are monthly cash-back features on travel websites like Expedia, where you can get up to 10% back. It's worth checking out (link below)

Basically, you subscribe to your streaming packages while in the US (like Hulu Live or YouTube TV), and then when you're overseas, you activate your VPN and log into your streaming account. Setting a VPN onto a streaming device (like Roku) is a bit more challenging as you'd probably need to bring your own wireless router and then set the VPN into the router. I didn't feel like doing that, so I just ran an HDMI cord from my computer to a television or projector.

One word of warning. NBC Peacock, for whatever reason, doesn't support HDMI sharing. In other words, if you plug your laptop directly into a TV via an HDMI cord the video feed will drop. Super annoying. A way around it, I've found, is to use a USB adapter. On my Mac, I have a USB connector that adds new ports to the computer (several USB, MicroSD, HDMI, and so on). When I run the HDMI through this adapter port and then plug it into the television Peacock works.

Peacock is the only streaming platform I've run into this problem with. Hulu, Disney+, Netflix, and Paramount all work just fine.

Q: I Own A Car That Isn't Fully Paid Off. What Should I Do?

I was in the same boat. I owned a truck but I still had six months worth of payments on it.

As you plan your departure, continue your monthly payments. Then, with a few weeks left, take your vehicle to local dealerships and receive quotes. Yes, you would likely make more money selling it independently, but there are two caveats to this. One, it can take a long time to sell it on your own. More importantly though, if a dealership buys the vehicle from you, they will pay off the remainder of your loan and cut you a check for the rest.

The fact of the matter is, that you can't independently sell your car if a bank has a lien on it. But dealerships have a workaround. So don't fret. As long as you owe less than the vehicle is worth, you'll be good to go.

I would recommend shopping around though. Go to different dealerships and compare prices. Chances are each will be comparable. But you never know. One dealership might give you enough extra to cover the first month of rent when you move.

Q: What Do Locals Think?

This is going to be a broad-term answer to the question. In almost any situation, wherever you move will be more affordable than the United States. Of course, his isn't always the case. There are some Asian and European countries where ou will pay more. But, typically, many people leave the U.S. because they can fford a better life elsewhere.

hat's the main reason I moved out.

ocals know that. It is pretty apparent to them you're likely from the United tates. When I was in Peru, everyone was glad I was there. Of course, Peruvians in eneral are incredibly friendly and helpful people. So even if they didn't want me here they likely would have still held a smile and been there to help. There also vasn't a massive expat or US immigration population, so nobody felt like they vere being pushed out of their homes because of foreigners moving in.

n Argentina, it was a little different. The majority of people were glad or ndifferent to me being there. But there were, I'd say 10 to 15 percent of people vho frankly wanted to blame me, and others like me, for the country's problems.)f course, that's not true. Really at all. But oftentimes people want someone to •lame, and it's easier to blame an outsider than to look internally. I bet you know t least one person in the United States who blames immigrants for many of the ountry's problems. It's no different.

hese individuals can be a vocal minority. If you post to social platforms like nstagram or TikTok they will undoubtedly find you and comment. As if they pend their entire day hunting videos and pictures like yours down.

Now, there are times when outsiders can be a burden. There are neighborhoods in ities like Mexico City and Lisbon where expats and immigrants with more noney have moved in, gobbled up real estate, and gentrified communities. This an shoot property values up and push locals out.

n this instance, there is a localized issue that is causing residents problems. 'ersonally, I try not to be like this. After all, I moved away from a country I could

no longer afford. I don't want to cause someone else to move because they can n
longer afford their own. So, if you do eventually want to purchase property i
your new home (where, at that point, when you're looking to make thin
permanent, you'd be considered an immigrant instead of an expat), I woul
recommend at least trying to be mindful of your surroundings and the loc
community.

The reality of everything is that, in some locations, everyone will be glad you'
there. They will want to share their culture with you. They will want you to sho
at the local markets and eat at their restaurants. They might find you exotic an
desire to show you off to all their friends. And then in some locations, a handf
of people might downright dislike you. Or at least resent you for having mo
freedom to work around.

Although, to me, freedom is more in the eye of the beholder. I went to colleg
took on $100K in student loan debt, and was instantly saddled with nearly $800
month payments. People in countries like Mexico or Argentina can attend loc
universities for free, and some of these universities are highly ranked in the worl
(in a recent report, the main universities in Mexico, Argentina, and Brazil wer
ranked higher than US institutions like University of Wisconsin, Michigan Stat
and North Carolina, so receiving a free bachelor's degree from the Latin America
schools can prove valuable). To me, having a bachelor's degree without paying
dime and the ability to move elsewhere (like Europe) with zero debt to my nam
sounded pretty great to me.

This is a longer answer to a short question. But basically, most people will like yo
some will resent you, and it's possible others will blame you for everything wron
with their country.

Helpful Resources

kuten:

ww.rakuten.com/r/GREYSO71?eeid=28187

Moving Abroad Checklist

In the Beginning

- Choosing a destination
- Secure remote work

Before Leaving

- Passport
- Renew credit/debit cards if expiring soon
- Secure credit card(s) with no foreign transaction fees
- Begin language courses (if necessary)

Driving

- International driver's license/permit
- Practice manual transmission driving (if necessary)

Phone Services

- Obtain a phone that supports both SIM and eSIM
- Sign up for WhatsApp
- Locate cheap wireless carrier/transfer your number to keep your current US number while living abroad

Connecting with Locals

- Facebook expat groups
- Dating applications (if single, naturally)

Handling Your Visa

- Determine particular visa requirements
- Begin securing documents
- Obtain FBI background check (if necessary)
- Consider consulting local immigration lawyer if you're confused/need help

Moving with Your Pet

- Identify airlines that can fly your pet (look at restrictions if you have a "dangerous" breed or a snubbed nosed dog).
- Receive all required vaccinations. Make sure your vet signs the documents in BLUE INK.
- Locate departure cities. If a layover is necessary look for a layover of between 2-3 hours. Many airlines will not allow pet layovers of longer than 4 (when flying in luggage).
- Obtain kennel based on transit and airline requirements.
- Replace plastic kennel screws with metal screws
- Purchase zip-ties and luggage locks for kennel

Things To Do Once You Arrive

- Secure local SIM card
- Follow up on any visa requirements
- Sign up for a gym (if desired). You may need to visit the doctor first.
- Celebrate your accomplishments!

Made in the USA
Las Vegas, NV
21 December 2023

83405274R00049